THE PLEASURE OF COOKING MINI SERIES

SPAIN

THE BOOK COMPANY

This English language edition
developed for and sold exclusively worldwide
by The Book Company

A Kevin Weldon Production

Published by Weldon Publishing
a division of Kevin Weldon & Associates Ltd
Level 5, 70 George St, Sydney 2000, Australia

First published 1992 as *The Complete Spanish Cookbook*
Reprinted in this edition for The Book Company 1992

© Copyright: Kevin Weldon and Associates Pty Limited 1992
© Copyright design: Kevin Weldon & Associates Pty Limited 1992

Printed in Singapore by Kyodo Printing Co (S'pore) Ltd

National Library of Australia Cataloguing-in-Publication Data

Spain.

Includes index.
ISBN 1 86302 223 6.

1. Cookery, Spanish. I. Passmore, Jacki. Complete Spanish cookbook. II. Title: Complete Spanish cookbook. (Series: Pleasure of cooking miniseries).

641.5946

WEIGHTS AND MEASURES

We have tested these recipes using standard
American cup and spoon measurements, and
have applied the following conversion.
3 cups = (750 ml/24 fl oz)   1 cup = (250 ml/8 fl oz)
1 quart = (1.14 l/40 fl oz)   1 tablespoon = (15 ml/½ fl oz)
½ cup = (120 ml/4 fl oz)

Photographs
Frontispiece: a selection of tapas includes center left,
   Calamares fritos (recipe page 7); top right, Buñuelitos de Jamón
   (recipe page 10); front, Gambas al Ajillo (recipe page 6)
Opposite title page: Paella Valenciana (recipe page 28)

CONTENTS

INTRODUCTION

The dramatic landscape of Spain's sweeping plateaux, fringed by rocky coastlines, reflects a history as turbulent, romantic and eventful as any to be found in Europe. This vibrant land occupies the bulk of the Iberian peninsula, curving into the Atlantic Ocean south of France, the rectangle of Portugal's land hugging its western periphery and the blue waters of the Mediterranean lapping its southern shores.

Spain is a many-faceted country, and its complexity intrigues. It's a land of extremes, of passion and spirit, of strongly held ideals, of a physical beauty that astounds, and of monuments that at once humble and amaze the viewer by their sheer number, age, size and artistry. Spain is a country of tremendous variation in landscape and terrain, in climate and culture. The people are proudly parochial or impressively sophisticated, always charmingly hospitable, and with physical characteristics revealing their richly blended ancestry. It's a country of many tongues, with four main languages—Basque, Catalan, Galician and *Castellano* (Castilian)—and many dialects. You may visit armed with your guidebook and parrot-phrasing of "useful" sentences only to find that *Castellano* is the second language in many parts. Spain's cuisine reflects all of these elements. It's intensely traditional and regional, yet today's chefs are boldly inventive, experimenting with new ingredients in age-old formulas, and new themes with foods that have been used for centuries. The layout of this book follows the geographical pattern of the provinces to provide a tantalizing array of diverse regional dishes.

The Spanish love to eat; they do it often, in quantity and with obvious relish. *Desayuno* (breakfast) is usually light—hot chocolate or coffee with *churros*, featherlight strips of freshly fried dough, or toast or pastries. (Eggs, bacon and cereal are for the hotel dining room.) At around 11 a.m. it's coffee again, with sweet buns. At 1 p.m., when shops and offices close for the afternoon break, many might slip into a bar for a quick drink and a nibble of *tapas* before heading home for a siesta or meeting friends in a restaurant for lunch. *La comida* (lunch) is to most Spanish people the main meal of the day. It is taken at leisure somewhere between 2 and 3 in the afternoon. It will be at least a 3-course meal, usually beginning with soup and bread or rolls followed by a fish or vegetable course and then a substantial main course. Dessert and coffee invariably follow. And of course there's wine! Little wonder that businesses do not begin trading again until around 4 p.m. And that is rather arbitrary; being "on time" is not high on the priority list here.

But the day's eating is only half through. *Merienda*—the Spanish answer to the British "afternoon tea"—means tea or coffee, cakes or pastries and light snacks taken in coffee shops and cafeterias at around 5 p.m. Then, as business closes for the evening somewhere between 7 and 9 p.m., it's back to the *tapas* bar for a drink and nibbles. Around 10 p.m., just when elsewhere one might be considering calling it a day, the restaurants once again open to an enthusiastic clientele for *la cena* (dinner/supper), again a 3- or 4-course production. The Spanish enjoy soups and often start a meal with one, but they also like egg dishes, simple fish courses such as a poached trout or a grilled fillet, salads or vegetables as first courses. In Spain the "three vegetables and meat" style of main course is not standard. You are more likely to receive your vegetables as a separate course, and the main course on its own with perhaps one vegetable as a garnish. After the evening meal, you might move on to another restaurant or coffee house for the sweet course and coffee.

If a country's eating habits are a reflection of the nation's character, then the Spanish are indeed an ebullient and fun-loving race.

TAPAS

OSTIONES A LA GADITANA
OYSTERS CÁDIZ STYLE

24 fresh oysters

1 teaspoon very finely chopped garlic

1 teaspoon very finely chopped parsley

$\frac{1}{3}$ teaspoon freshly cracked black pepper

$\frac{1}{4}$ teaspoon hot paprika

3 tablespoons fine dry breadcrumbs

olive oil

lemon wedges

Remove the top shells from the oysters and loosen oysters from their lower shell. Arrange on a baking sheet. Evenly dress them with garlic, parsley, pepper and paprika, then cover each with a fine coating of breadcrumbs. Add a few drops of oil and place in a very hot oven or under the broiler/grill until they are well warmed. Serve with lemon wedges.

GAMBAS AL AJILLO
GARLIC SHRIMP (PRAWNS)

24 medium-size shrimp (prawns) in the shell

$\frac{2}{3}$ cup/150 ml/5 fl oz mild olive oil

5-6 cloves garlic, finely chopped

lemon wedges

Remove heads from shrimp if desired, although usually they are left whole. Heat oil to smoking point. Sauté the shrimp with garlic over fairly high heat until they turn pink, about 2 minutes. Serve immediately with bread for dunking or on a bed of boiled rice. Garnish with lemon wedges.

CALAMARES FRITOS
FRIED SQUID

10-12 fresh squid, skinned, cleaned

1 teaspoon sweet paprika

$\frac{1}{3}$ teaspoon cayenne pepper

1 teaspoon salt

$\frac{1}{4}$ teaspoon black pepper

1 cup/120 g/4 oz all-purpose (plain) flour

2 eggs, beaten

3 cups/750 ml/24 fl oz olive or vegetable oil

lemon wedges

Cut the squid into narrow rings and dry on paper towels. Place paprika, cayenne, salt, pepper and flour in a paper bag. Add squid and flour lightly and evenly, then remove, dip into egg and flour again. Heat oil to smoking point, then reduce heat slightly. Fry the squid in small handfuls for about 20 seconds only, and remove on a slotted spoon or strainer. Drain well on absorbent paper before serving hot with lemon for squeezing.

GAMBAS REBOZADAS
FRIED SHRIMP (PRAWNS)

12 medium-size fresh shrimp (prawns) in the shell

$\frac{1}{2}$ cup/60 g/2 oz all-purpose (plain) flour

1 large egg, beaten

ice water

4 cups/1 l/32 fl oz deep frying oil

salt, pepper and paprika

Peel the shrimp, leaving the tails in place. Slit down center backs and remove the intestinal vein. Rinse and dry the shrimp. Make a thick but creamy batter with the flour, egg and ice water. Heat oil in a wide pan. Dip shrimp into the batter, then fry in the oil until golden. Remove with a skimmer and drain on paper towels. Sprinkle with salt, pepper and paprika and serve hot.

7

TORTILLA
SPANISH OMELETTE

5 tablespoons olive oil

3 large potatoes, peeled and thinly
sliced

1 medium onion, very thinly
sliced

6 eggs, lightly beaten

salt and black pepper

In a non-stick 9-inch/23-cm pan heat half the oil and fry the potatoes until tender and only very lightly colored; it is vital that the potatoes do not become crisp and dry at the edges. Remove or push to one side of the pan. Fry the onion until soft and lightly golden. Remove from the pan with a slotted spoon and mix the potatoes and onion into the eggs, adding salt and pepper. Reheat the pan with the remaining oil and, when it is very hot, pour in the *tortilla* mixture. Reduce the heat and cook gently until the underside is golden and firm. Use a spatula no more than $1\frac{1}{2}$ inches/4 cm wide to shape the edge of the *tortilla* as it cooks so that it is of even thickness right across, not tapering off at its perimeter. Select a plate the same size as the tortilla, fitting inside the rim of the pan. Place it directly on the *tortilla.* Invert the pan so the omelette is transferred to the plate, then return the pan to the heat. Slide the omelette back in to cook the other side; cook gently until it feels firm to the touch. Invert again or slide onto a serving plate and cut into wedges to serve.

CANAPÉS DE FIAMBRES
HORS D'OEUVRES

1 small baguette

olive oil (optional)

24 anchovy fillets in oil, drained

strips of pimiento, drained

Slice the baguette and toast or fry in olive oil. Roll each anchovy around a strip of pimiento and pierce with a toothpick. Place on the toast and serve.

Tortillitas de Gambas
LITTLE SHRIMP (PRAWN) PATTIES

12 oz/375 g small peeled shrimp
(prawns), finely chopped

1 small onion, finely chopped

1 clove garlic, finely chopped

1 tablespoon finely chopped
parsley

$1\frac{1}{2}$ cups/180 g/6 oz all-purpose
(plain) flour

1 teaspoon baking powder

salt and black pepper

$\frac{1}{4}$ teaspoon hot paprika or chili
powder

1 tablespoon dry sherry

4 cups/1 l/32 fl oz olive or
vegetable oil

Mix the shrimp, onion, garlic and parsley. Sift the flour, baking powder, salt, pepper and paprika into a bowl; add the sherry and enough water to make a creamy batter. Stir in the shrimp mixture. Heat the oil in a wide pan and fry spoonfuls of the mixture until crisp and golden. Remove with a skimmer and drain on paper towels. Serve hot.

Emparedados de Jamón y Espárragos
FRIED HAM AND ASPARAGUS ROLLS

8 stalks green or white asparagus

8 small, thin slices cooked or
cured ham

salt and pepper

2 eggs, beaten

1 cup/120 g/4 oz fine dry
breadcrumbs

1 cup/250 ml/4 fl oz olive oil

Place an asparagus stalk in the center of each slice of ham and roll up. Secure with toothpicks and season with salt and pepper. Dip into the egg and coat with crumbs. Fry in the hot oil until crumbs are golden. Serve at once.

Variation: Make these also with paper-thin slices of veal wrapped around the ham and asparagus.

9

HIGADITOS
LITTLE LIVER STICKS

12 oz/370 g calves' liver

salt and pepper

1 teaspoon sweet paprika

1 tablespoon dry sherry

1 cup/120 g/4 oz all-purpose
(plain) flour

2 cups/500 ml/16 oz olive or
vegetable oil

1 dried red chili, seeded and very
finely chopped

1 teaspoon chopped garlic

2-3 teaspoons chopped parsley

Cut the liver into bite-size cubes, peeling off any fragments of skin. Season with salt, pepper and paprika, then sprinkle on the sherry. Roll in flour.

Fry in the oil until golden brown and cooked through. Drain off the oil and toss the liver with chopped chili, garlic and parsley for a few seconds. Serve.

BUÑUELITOS DE JAMÓN
HAM FRITTERS

4 oz/120 g *jamón serrano*, very
finely diced

1 tablespoon olive oil

1 small onion, very finely diced

2 teaspoons chopped parsley

pinch each of salt and pepper

$\frac{1}{2}$ cup/60 g/2 oz all-purpose (plain)
flour

$\frac{1}{2}$ teaspoon baking powder

2 egg whites, beaten to a froth

$\frac{1}{3}$–$\frac{1}{2}$ cup/90–120 ml/3–4 fl oz water

2 cups/500 ml/16 fl oz olive or
vegetable oil

Sauté the ham in the oil until well colored, add the onion and fry until golden. Remove from the heat and stir in the parsley and seasoning. Beat flour and baking powder with the egg whites and water to make a smoother batter of pouring consistency. Let it stand for 20 minutes. Stir in the ham. Heat the oil almost to smoking point, then reduce heat slightly. Drop spoonfuls of the batter into the oil to fry until golden, turning once. Remove with a slotted spoon and drain well. Serve hot.

Champiñones Rellenos con Picadillo
STUFFED MUSHROOMS

12 medium-size fresh button
mushrooms

1 green (spring) onion/shallot or
scallion, minced

1 hard-boiled egg, minced

2 teaspoons heavy cream

salt and pepper

1 egg, beaten

$\frac{1}{2}$ cup/60 g/2 oz all-purpose (plain)
flour

2 cups/500 ml/16 fl oz olive oil

Pull off mushroom stems and chop very finely. Mix with the onion, egg, cream, salt and pepper and stuff into the mushroom caps. Dip into beaten egg and coat lightly with flour. Fry in oil until golden. Serve with toothpicks.

Ciruelas Rellenas
STUFFED PRUNES

24 unpitted prunes

1 small onion, very finely chopped

90 g/3 oz bacon, very finely
chopped

$1\frac{1}{2}$ tablespoons olive oil

3 chicken livers, chopped

salt and pepper

$1\frac{1}{2}$ teaspoons very finely chopped
parsley

6 very thin slices *jamón serrano,*
bacon or prosciutto

Make a slit in one end of each prune and squeeze out the pit. Sauté the onion and chopped bacon in the oil until softened. Add the livers and sauté until they change color, mashing with the back of a spoon. Add salt and pepper with parsley and mix well. Press a small amount of the filling into each prune. Cut the ham or bacon slices in half lengthwise, then cut each piece in half crosswise to make 24 pieces. Wrap a piece around each prune and secure with a toothpick. Place on a baking sheet and bake in a preheated 425°F/220°C/Gas 8 oven for about 5 minutes if using ham, 7 to 8 minutes if using bacon. Serve hot.

MADRID, LA MANCHA AND NEW CASTILE

Sopa de Ajo
GARLIC SOUP

8 cloves garlic, peeled

$\frac{1}{4}$ cup/60 ml/2 fl oz olive oil

8 very thin slices coarse country-
style bread, crusts trimmed

$1\frac{1}{2}$ teaspoons sweet paprika

6 cups/1.5 l/1$\frac{1}{2}$ qt veal or chicken
stock

salt and pepper

3 eggs

chopped parsley

SERVES 6

Fry the whole garlic cloves in oil until they are very well colored and the flavor has impregnated the oil, then discard. Fry the bread until crisp. Remove and set aside. Add paprika to the oil and fry briefly, then add the stock, salt and pepper and bring to a boil. Break up the bread, return to the soup and simmer for about 10 minutes. Transfer to an ovenproof serving dish. Beat the eggs and pour slowly into the soup without stirring; they should rise to the surface. Place in a preheated 450°F/220°C/Gas 8 oven until the eggs have cooked to a firm layer on top. Sprinkle parsley on top and serve at once.

Torta de Anchoas
ANCHOVY TOAST

4 thick slices country-style bread

1 large ripe tomato

48 anchovy fillets packed in oil,
drained

SERVES 4 (*TAPA*)

Lightly toast the bread and rub with the cut tomato. Arrange the anchovies diagonally across the bread. Cut in halves to serve.

Tortilla (recipe page 8)

Right, Pierna de Cabrito Asado (recipe page 6)
Front left, Roscos (recipe page 17)
Remaining dishes comprise Callos a la Madrileña (recipe page 13); rice soup,
cabbage and sausage; meat and garbanzos; and a side dish of spicy tomato
sauce

Pollo en Escabeche (recipe page 15)

CALLOS A LA MADRILEÑA
TRIPE MADRID STYLE

1 lb/500 g veal shank/shin

1 pig's foot/trotter

1 bay leaf

2 medium onions, chopped

6 whole black peppercorns

1 whole clove

1½ lb/750 g tripe

3 cloves garlic, sliced

2 tablespoons olive oil

6 oz/180 g *chorizo* sausage, sliced

2 oz/60 g *tocino* or other cured ham

1 tablespoon sweet paprika

1 cup/250 ml/8 fl oz dry white wine

2 teaspoons tomato paste

1 fresh hot red chili pepper, seeded and chopped

1 sprig fresh thyme

1 sprig fresh parsley

1 *morcilla* or other blood sausage, about 3 oz/90 g, sliced

SERVES 4–6 (*TAPA*)

Blanch the veal and pig's foot in boiling water and drain. Place in a large pan and cover with water. Add the bay leaf and half the onion, the peppercorns, clove and tripe. Bring to a boil, reduce heat and simmer, partially covered, for 2 hours. Strain the stock into another pan. Remove meat from the veal shank and cut into small pieces. Set aside. Cut tripe into 1½-inch/5-cm squares. Place the shank bone and pig's foot in the stock and add the tripe. Sauté the remaining onion and the garlic in the oil for 2 to 3 minutes, add the *chorizo* and *tocino* and fry for another 2 to 3 minutes. Add the paprika and cook for a few seconds, then add the wine and tomato paste. Stir to mix well, then pour over the tripe and add the chili and herbs. Cover and simmer for 1 hour.

Remove the shank bones and discard. Remove the pig's foot, scrape off skin and cut the meat into small pieces. Return shank and pork to the pan and add the *morcilla* sausage. Simmer for another hour, or until the tripe is very tender. Add salt and pepper to taste. Serve hot.

ALBÓNDIGAS DE TERNERA CON SALSA DE TOMATE
VEAL MEATBALLS IN TOMATO SAUCE

4 oz/120 g lean veal, diced

2 oz/60 g chopped ham

2 oz/60 g chopped salted *tocino* or smoked bacon

pinch each of salt, pepper and nutmeg

2 eggs*

2 tablespoons all-purpose (plain) flour

1 cup/120 g/4 oz fine dry breadcrumbs (optional)

1 cup/250 ml/8 fl oz olive oil

1 recipe fresh tomato sauce (page 386)

SERVES 4 (*TAPA*)

Place the meats with seasonings in a food processor and grind to a smooth paste. Add 1 egg and process briefly, then form into small balls and coat lightly with flour. Dip into beaten egg and roll in breadcrumbs, if used. Fry in the oil until golden brown and cooked through. Drain. Heat the tomato sauce, add the meatballs and serve.

*Only one egg is needed if the meatballs are not to be coated with crumbs.

SALSA DE TOMATE
FRESH TOMATO SAUCE

1 large onion, very finely chopped

3 tablespoons olive oil

3 cloves garlic, very finely chopped

5 large sun-ripened tomatoes, peeled, seeded and chopped

1¼ teaspoons salt

⅓ teaspoon black pepper

1 tablespoon chopped fresh herbs (parsley, rosemary, thyme, oregano)

MAKES 3-3½ CUPS

Sauté the onion in the oil until soft and very lightly colored. Add the garlic and sauté briefly, then add the tomato and cook slowly until reduced to a pulp. Season with salt and pepper and add the herbs. Simmer briefly, then pass through a sieve or purée in a food processor or blender if a smooth sauce is desired. Can be frozen.

CEBOLLITAS CON PASAS
BABY ONIONS WITH RAISINS

$1\frac{1}{2}$ lb/750 g small onions, peeled

2 medium tomatoes, chopped

$\frac{1}{2}$ cup/120 ml/4 fl oz red wine
vinegar

$\frac{1}{3}$ cup/90 g/3 oz sugar

$\frac{3}{4}$ cup/110 g/$3\frac{1}{2}$ oz raisins

1 bouquet garni

$\frac{1}{4}$ cup/60 ml/2 fl oz virgin olive oil
(or butter)

salt and pepper

SERVES 4

Combine all ingredients in a casserole. Cover and cook
in a 350°F/180°C/Gas 4 oven for 1 hour, stirring from
time to time and adding a little extra liquid if needed.

POLLO EN ESCABECHE
MARINATED CHICKEN

3 lb/1.5-kg chicken

$\frac{1}{4}$ cup/60 ml/2 fl oz olive oil

3 cloves garlic, peeled

1 teaspoon black peppercorns

1 bay leaf, crumbled

1 teaspoon salt

$2\frac{1}{2}$ cups/650 ml/21 fl oz dry white
wine

$\frac{3}{4}$ cup/180 ml/6 fl oz white wine or
cider vinegar

1 lemon, sliced

SERVES 4–6

Cut the chicken into 4 pieces. Dry with paper towels
and fry in the oil until lightly colored without allowing
the surface to become crusty. Transfer to a non-aluminum pan and add the remaining ingredients. Bring just
to a boil, then reduce heat to very low and simmer for
at least 1 hour. Allow to cool, then place in an earthenware or glass dish, cover with plastic wrap and chill.
Serve cold with a little of the cooking liquid.

CHULETAS DE TERNERA
VEAL CUTLETS CASTILIAN STYLE

3 cloves garlic, mashed

12 small veal cutlets

salt and pepper

1 tablespoon olive oil

SERVES 4

Spread the garlic evenly over the cutlets, then season with salt and pepper. Brush lightly with olive oil. Arrange on a rack in a roasting pan. Roast in a 450°F/230°C/Gas 6 oven for 10 minutes, then turn and roast the other side until cooked to preference. Separately roast small cubes of potato with plenty of pan drippings and serve with the cutlets.

PIERNA DE CABRITO ASADO
ROAST LEG OF KID

4- to 5-lb/2- to 2.5-kg leg of kid

3 cloves garlic, mashed

salt

3 tablespoons lard

3 sprigs fresh rosemary

1 cup/250 ml/8 fl oz Spanish brandy or dry sherry

1 tablespoon (plain) all-purpose flour

pepper

SERVES 6

Trim any loose fragments of fat or meat from the leg. Place in a rack in a roasting pan. Make a paste of the garlic and salt and rub into the leg, then spread with the lard. Place the rosemary in the pan and add 2 cups/ 500 ml/16 fl oz water. Roast in a 400°F/200°C/Gas 8 oven for 15 minutes. Reduce heat to 350°F/180°C/Gas 4 and roast for a further 1¼ hours or until done to preference, turning the roast every 15 minutes and pouring the brandy over the roast halfway through cooking.

Let the roast stand on a cutting board for at least 10 minutes before carving. Skim off fat and boil up the pan juices. Sprinkle on flour, and cook, stirring, until the gravy thickens. Season with salt and pepper; discard the rosemary. If desired, add extra brandy or sherry to the gravy just before serving.

ROSCOS
DOUGHNUT CAKES

1 cup/250 ml/8 fl oz flavorless
vegetable oil

1 tablespoon aniseed

4 cups/500 g/1 lb all-purpose
(plain) flour

$\frac{1}{4}$ teaspoon salt

1 cup/250 ml/8 fl oz dry white
wine

$\frac{1}{3}$ cup/90 g/3 oz sugar

3 medium eggs, well beaten

confectioners' (icing) sugar or
frosting (below)

Frosting:

$\frac{1}{2}$ cup/120 g/4 oz superfine sugar

2 teaspoons lemon juice

2 tablespoons water

1 egg white

1 tablespoon confectioners' (icing)
sugar

MAKES 24

Heat the oil and aniseed together in a small saucepan for 5 minutes, then let cool. Sift the flour and salt into a mixing bowl. Add the wine, aniseed oil and sugar and mix lightly. Gradually add the egg, beating with a wooden spoon to form a smooth dough. Turn out onto a lightly floured board and knead until the dough is smooth and elastic. Cover with plastic wrap and let stand for at least 2 hours. Divide into 24 pieces and roll each out into a thin sausage shape. Twist into rings and pinch the ends together. Place on a greased and floured baking sheet. Bake in a preheated 375°F/190°C/Gas 5 oven for about 20 minutes or until the buns feel dry and springy on the surface. Remove to a cake cooling rack.

Dissolve the sugar in a small saucepan with lemon juice and water. Cook until it forms a syrup, then cool. Beat the egg white until stiff, pour on the syrup in a thin stream and beat in, adding the confectioners' sugar. Spread the prepared frosting over the cakes.

EXTREMADURA AND ANDALUSIA

GAZPACHO SEVILLANO
SEVILLE STYLE GAZPACHO

1 green bell pepper (capsicum),
seeded and chopped

1 medium onion, chopped

1–2 cloves garlic, peeled

$\frac{1}{2}$ cucumber, peeled, seeded and
chopped

3 large sun-ripened tomatoes,
peeled and seeded

6 toasted blanched almonds

1 large slice white bread (crusts
trimmed), soaked in water and
squeezed dry

1 teaspoon salt

1 tablespoon chopped fresh herbs
(preferably parsley and mint)

$\frac{1}{2}$ cup/120 ml/4 fl oz virgin olive oil

6 cups/1.5 l/1$\frac{1}{2}$ qt ice water

3–4 tablespoons sherry vinegar

SERVES 6

Place the vegetables and 1 cup/250 ml/8 fl oz water in a food processor or blender and process briefly until smooth. Strain through a nylon sieve into a soup bowl. Process the almonds, bread, salt and half the herbs to a paste, adding the oil. Add some of the ice water, then strain into the puréed vegetables and add the vinegar and remaining water. Chill thoroughly.

Variations: Additional green peppers, olives, onion, cucumber and tomato, cut into very small dice, as well as chopped hard-boiled eggs and croutons of day-old bread fried in olive oil, are served separately to be added to taste.

HUEVOS A LA FLAMENCA
GYPSY EGGS

$\frac{3}{4}$ cup/180 ml/6 fl oz olive oil

2 large potatoes, peeled and cubed

4 thin slices *jamón serrano* or other cured ham, cut into narrow strips*

1 medium onion, thinly sliced

2 large sun-ripened tomatoes, peeled, seeded and sliced

1 small red bell pepper (capsicum), seeded and sliced

12 green beans, halved crosswise

12 slender green asparagus stalks, halved crosswise

1 tablespoon tomato paste (optional)

salt and pepper

1 *chorizo* sausage, sliced

4 large eggs

2 teaspoons chopped herbs (parsley, thyme, marjoram)

SERVES 4

Heat the olive oil in a shallow ovenproof sauté pan or paella pan and sauté the potatoes until golden on all sides. Pour off about $\frac{2}{3}$ of the oil, add the ham and onion to the pan and cook over medium heat for 2 to 3 minutes. Add tomatoes and cook to soften, then add peppers, reserving some for garnish. Add beans and asparagus and cook over low heat until vegetables are almost tender, stirring carefully with a flat spatula once or twice. Mix tomato paste with a little water and pour over the dish. Add salt, pepper, herbs and the sliced sausage and cook another 2 to 3 minutes. Make 4 depressions in the mixture and slide in the eggs. Arrange reserved peppers on top. Bake in a preheated 350°F/180°C/Gas 4 oven for about 12 minutes or until the eggs are just cooked. Garnish with remaining peppers and serve at once.

*Thinly sliced prosciutto is excellent in this dish. Cut into short strips and add to the vegetable mixture before placing in the oven.

Variation: *Huevos a la flamenca* can be cooked in individual ramekins to serve as a first course or supper dish. Cook the vegetables and ham as above, and spoon into small ovenproof dishes. Break an egg on top of each and decorate with the sliced sausage and peppers. Bake for about 10 minutes.

19

Ensalada Sevillana
SEVILLE SALAD

1 large head chicory (curly endive)

2 Belgian endive (witloof), leaves
separated

1½ cups/8 oz/250 g small pitted
black olives

1 tablespoon chopped fresh
tarragon

2 tablespoons wine vinegar

⅓ cup/90 ml/3 fl oz virgin olive oil

salt

1 clove garlic, mashed

SERVES 4

Rinse the chicory, shake dry and separate leaves. Cut
larger leaves into pieces. Place in a salad bowl with the
endive leaves, olives and tarragon. Whisk the vinegar,
oil, salt and garlic together until thoroughly emulsified.
Pour over the salad, toss and serve.

Variation: Tart Seville oranges, thinly sliced, and rings
of red Spanish or salad onion make an interesting
addition.

Pez Espada Frito
FRIED SWORDFISH STEAKS

4 swordfish steaks, about 7 oz/
200 g each

4 cloves garlic, finely chopped

½ cup/120 ml/4 fl oz olive oil

juice of 1 large lemon

¾ cup/90 g/3 oz all-purpose (plain)
flour

2 teaspoons chopped parsley

sliced lemon and orange

SERVES 4

Place the swordfish steaks in a flat dish and add the
garlic, 2 tablespoons of the olive oil and lemon juice.
Marinate for 15 minutes, then turn and marinate a
further 10 minutes. Drain and coat lightly with flour.
Fry in the remaining oil for about 3 minutes on each
side. Garnish with chopped parsley and the sliced lemon
and orange and serve with boiled potatoes.

Variation: Cut the fish into cubes and thread onto oiled
skewers with pieces of onion and bell pepper (capsicum).
Marinate, then grill over charcoal until done.

CAZUELITAS DE ESPÁRRAGOS TRIGUEROS
LITTLE CASSEROLES OF WILD ASPARAGUS

48 stems (2 bunches/1½ lbs/750 g)
espárragos trigueros or other
asparagus

1 teaspoon salt

½ cup/120 ml/4 fl oz olive oil

1 slice white bread, crusts
trimmed

2 cloves garlic, finely chopped

1 tablespoon sweet paprika

black pepper

1 tablespoon red wine vinegar

6 eggs

1 teaspoon finely chopped parsley

SERVES 6

Trim the asparagus and cut into 2-inch/5-cm lengths. Cook in boiling salted water for 4 minutes; drain. Heat the oil and fry bread until golden. Remove, then fry the garlic until lightly colored. Add the paprika and pepper. Transfer contents of the pan to a food processor, breaking up the bread into small pieces.

Process to crumbs. Divide the asparagus among 4 small earthenware ramekins and sprinkle with the crumbs. Drizzle on the vinegar and break an egg over each. Sprinkle with parsley. Bake in a very hot oven for about 5 minutes or until the eggs are just set. Serve at once.

Riñones a la Jerezana
KIDNEYS IN A RICH SHERRY SAUCE

2 lb/1 kg veal kidneys

$\frac{3}{4}$ cup/180 ml/6 fl oz milk

1 cup/250 ml/8 fl oz olive oil

salt and pepper

1 cup/250 ml/8 fl oz amontillado
or fino sherry

6 cloves garlic, minced

1 medium onion, finely chopped

1 tablespoon all-purpose (plain)
flour

1 bay leaf

1 large sun-ripened tomato,
peeled, seeded and chopped

$\frac{3}{4}$ cup/180 ml/6 fl oz veal or beef
stock

2 teaspoons tomato paste

$\frac{1}{4}$ teaspoon nutmeg

1 tablespoon finely chopped
parsley

2 slices white bread, crusts
trimmed

SERVES 6

Place kidneys in a bowl, cover with the milk and set aside for 2 hours. Drain and rinse. Cut in halves and use kitchen shears to remove the fat. Cut kidneys into bite-sized cubes. Heat $\frac{1}{4}$ cup/60 ml/2 fl oz olive oil in a wide pan until almost smoking. Add the kidneys and sauté until they change color. Add salt and pepper and the sherry. Cook over high heat for 2 minutes, then remove the kidneys with a slotted spoon and continue to boil the sherry until reduced by $\frac{2}{3}$. Pour over the kidneys. Add another 2 tablespoons oil to the pan and fry the garlic and onion until lightly colored. Sprinkle on the flour and cook, stirring, until golden. Add the bay leaf, tomato, stock, tomato paste and nutmeg and bring to a boil, stirring; cook 2 to 3 minutes. Return the kidneys and their liquid, add salt and pepper to taste and half the parsley. Simmer for about 5 minutes, or until the kidneys are tender and sauce is thick. Cut the bread into quarters and fry in the remaining oil. Pile the kidneys into the center of a serving plate and surround with the toast. Sprinkle on remaining parsley.

POLVORONES SEVILLANOS
SEVILLIAN SHORTBREAD

1 cup/250 g/8 oz lard or
margarine

½ cup/90 g/3 oz confectioners'
(icing) sugar

1 egg

1 tablespoon orange liqueur

1 tablespoon finely grated orange
peel (rind)

3½ cups/420 g/14 oz all-purpose
(plain) flour, sifted

small pinch of salt

MAKES ABOUT 20

Cream the lard or margarine in a mixing bowl and beat
in the sugar. Add the egg, liqueur and peel, then slowly
work in the flour and salt. Do not overwork the mixture
or it will become oily. Turn onto a floured board and
roll out to about ⅔ inch/2 cm thickness. Use a floured
small round cookie (biscuit) cutter to cut out the cookies.
Use up the trimmings by rerolling and cutting out in
the same way. Place on a greased and floured cookie
(biscuit) pan cook in a preheated hot oven 400°F/200°C/
Gas 6 for about 24 minutes. The cookies should be very
lightly browned on top when done. Transfer to a rack
to cool.

Tip: Dust with confectioners' (icing) sugar before serving,
or pipe on thin lines of chocolate.

HIGOS CON DULCE DE MÁLAGA
FIGS IN MÁLAGA WINE

16 dried figs

1½ cups/400 ml/13 fl oz Málaga
wine or tokay, muscat or sweet
sherry

2 tablespoons confectioners'
(icing) sugar

SERVES 4

Snip off the stem from each fig and place figs in a glass
dish. Pour on the wine and marinate overnight. Drain,
reserving the wine for another use. Sprinkle figs with
confectioners' sugar and serve immediately with
whipped cream or ice cream.

MURCIA AND VALENCIA (THE LEVANTE)

Sardinas a la Murciana
SARDINES WITH TOMATOES IN A CASSEROLE

24 small fresh sardines, about
1½ lb/750 g

5 large sun-ripened tomatoes,
sliced

1 large onion, sliced

1 large potato, peeled and very
thinly sliced

1 green bell pepper (capsicum),
seeded and sliced

3 cloves garlic, sliced

2 tablespoons chopped parsley

salt and pepper

2 tablespoons olive oil

2 tablespoons fresh breadcrumbs

1–2 teaspoons chopped fresh
herbs

SERVES 6

Clean and rinse fish thoroughly. Remove fillets, leaving backbones attached to heads; discard bones or reserve for making fish stock. Coat a casserole generously with olive oil. Place ⅓ of the tomato in the casserole, followed by half the onion, potato and pepper. Arrange half the fish evenly over the top. Scatter on garlic and parsley and season generously with salt and pepper. Add more tomato and repeat layering, then spread remaining tomato on top and season with salt and pepper. Drizzle half of the olive oil evenly over the casserole. Bake in a preheated 350°F/180°C/Gas 4 oven for about 50 minutes; after 30 minutes, remove the foil and sprinkle on bread-crumbs mixed with the chopped herbs and the remaining olive oil.

Cazuelitas de Espárragos Trigueros (recipe page 21)

Empanadas Valencianas (recipe page 25)

Empanadas Valencianas
STUFFED SAVORY PASTRIES

1 recipe empanada/empanadilla
pastry (page 383)

1 leek, trimmed, rinsed and
chopped

1 large clove garlic, minced

2 tablespoons olive oil

2 small very ripe tomatoes,
peeled, seeded and chopped

4 oz/120 g *jamón serrano* or other
cured ham*, very finely diced

2 hard-boiled eggs, chopped

1 tablespoon finely chopped
parsley

salt and pepper

1 egg, beaten

MAKES 6

Prepare the dough and set aside. Sauté the leek with garlic in the oil until softened, add tomato and cook briefly. Add the ham and sauté briefly, then remove from the pan and let cool.

Mix chopped eggs and parsley into filling, seasoning to taste. Roll out the dough thinly and use a circular cutter to make 6 rounds of pastry. Place a portion of filling to one side of each, leaving the edge uncovered. Use a small brush to moisten the edges with water, then fold over and pinch or crimp the edges to seal. Prick tops with a fork or skewer. Brush with beaten egg and place on a greased baking sheet. Bake in a preheated 400°F/200°C/Gas 6 oven for about 25 minutes or until the tops are golden brown.

Empanada Dough

2 cups/250 g/8 oz all-purpose (plain) flour

$\frac{1}{2}$ teaspoon salt

1 tablespoon Pernod

$\frac{1}{3}$ cup/90 ml/3 fl oz olive oil
ice water

Enough for 6 large or 36–48 small empanadas

Sift the flour and salt onto a board and make a well in the center. Add the Pernod and olive oil, cover with flour and work partially in. Add enough ice water to make a smooth but reasonably firm dough. Knead lightly, then wrap in plastic and set aside for at least 1 hour before using.

CEBOLLITAS AL HORNO
BAKED BABY ONIONS

16 small onions, peeled

3 tablespoons olive oil

2 tablespoons dry white wine

1 tablespoon white wine vinegar

3 cloves garlic, finely chopped

$2\frac{1}{2}$ teaspoons sweet paprika

salt and pepper

SERVES 4

Cut the tops from the onions and flatten the bases without cutting so deeply that they fall apart. Stand in a small baking dish and add the oil, wine and vinegar. Sprinkle the garlic, paprika, salt and pepper evenly over the onions and cover the dish with perforated aluminum foil. Bake in a preheated 350°F/180°C/Gas 4 oven for about 40 minutes, basting twice and uncovering in the final 10 minutes to crisp the surface.

CHULETAS DE CORDERO EN AJO CABAÑIL
LAMB CUTLETS WITH GARLIC

12–18 well-trimmed lamb cutlets

$\frac{1}{2}$ cup/120 ml/4 fl oz olive oil

4 medium potatoes, peeled and sliced on a mandolin

4–7 cloves garlic, finely chopped

$1\frac{1}{4}$ teaspoons hot paprika

$1\frac{1}{2}$ tablespoons red wine vinegar

salt and pepper

SERVES 6

Fry the cutlets in the oil in a wide pan until evenly browned on the surface and still slightly pink in the center, about 7 minutes. Remove and set aside. In the same pan fry the potatoes until crisp and golden. Arrange the cutlets on top. Mix the garlic and paprika and moisten with the vinegar. Add salt and pepper and pour over the dish. Serve at once.

Tip: If preferred, the garlic can be sautéed in olive oil until just golden.

ARROZ CON POLLO
RICE WITH CHICKEN

3-lb/1.5-kg chicken

salt and pepper

$\frac{1}{2}$ cup/120 ml/4 fl oz olive oil

3 oz/90 g *chorizo* sausage, sliced

2 oz/60 g *jamón serrano* or other
cured ham, diced

1 green bell pepper (capsicum),
seeded and diced

1 medium onion, chopped

3 cloves garlic, finely chopped

1 small fresh hot red chili pepper,
chopped

2 large very ripe tomatoes, peeled,
seeded and chopped

1 teaspoon tomato paste

2 cups/400 g/14 oz short-grain/
round white rice

3 cups/750 ml/24 fl oz chicken
stock or water

1 cup/250 ml/8 fl oz dry white
wine

$\frac{1}{4}$ teaspoon powdered saffron

1–2 tablespoons chopped parsley

SERVES 4–6

Cut the chicken into small serving pieces and season
with salt and pepper. Brown in the oil in a wide skillet
or *paella* pan for about 8 minutes, then remove. Sauté
the sausage and ham briefly, then add the pepper, onion,
garlic and chili and sauté until the onion has softened.
Add tomatoes and paste and cook for 5 minutes, then
add the rice and mix in well.

Bring the stock to a boil and pour over the rice, cooking
over high heat for about 3 minutes. Add wine and reduce
temperature to low. Cook, stirring to prevent the rice
from sticking to the pan, until the liquid is below the
level of the rice. Mix saffron with $\frac{1}{2}$ cup/120 ml/4 fl oz
boiling water, pour over the rice and stir in with half
the parsley. Arrange the chicken over the rice and bake
in a preheated 400°F/200°C/Gas 6 oven for about
25 minutes or until the chicken is cooked through and
the rice is fluffy. Garnish with the remaining parsley.

PAELLA VALENCIANA
VALENCIA STYLE RICE

1 lb/500 g chicken meat
(preferably from the thigh)

8 oz/250 g lean pork

salt

$\frac{1}{2}$ cup/120 ml/4 fl oz olive oil

1 large tomato, skinned, seeded
and chopped

3 cloves garlic, peeled and
chopped

$\frac{2}{3}$ teaspoon sweet paprika

$\frac{1}{2}$ cup/90 g/3 oz shelled fresh peas

$\frac{1}{2}$ cup/120 g/4 fl oz sliced green
beans

12 prepared fresh or canned snails

$2\frac{1}{2}$ cups/300 g/10 oz short round-
grain white rice

6 cups/1.5 l/1$\frac{1}{2}$ qt boiling water*

8–10 threads saffron

salt and pepper

12 clams in the shell, cleaned and
soaked

6 mussels in the shell, cleaned and
soaked

3 small squid, cleaned and cut
into rings

6 small *langostinos* or large shrimp
(prawns) or scampi

halved lemons

SERVES 6

Cut the chicken into small pieces and pork into bite-
sized cubes. Season with salt and brown in olive oil in
a *paella* or other suitable large wide flat pan. Add the
tomato, garlic and paprika, and stir on medium heat for
2 minutes. Stir in the peas, beans and snails, then the
rice and cook briefly. Add half the boiling water and
cook until it is partially absorbed into the rice. Crush
the saffron with 2 tablespoons of the boiling water and
stir into the rice with salt and pepper. Add half the
remaining hot water (or stock) to the rice and cook until
partially absorbed. Place the clams, mussels, squid and
langostinos or other shellfish on top of the rice and cook
until rice is tender, adding the remaining liquid as needed.
When the dish is done the rice should still be quite moist
and should be chewy-tender. Stir seafood into the *paella*
and serve in the pan with halved lemons.

CATALONIA AND THE BALEARIC ISLANDS

TUMBRET
MALLORCA VEGETABLE FLAN

2 medium eggplants (aubergines),
thinly sliced

salt

2 large potatoes, peeled and sliced

½ cup/120 ml/4 fl oz olive oil

2 green bell peppers (capsicums),
seeded and sliced

5 cloves garlic, peeled and
chopped

1 medium onion, chopped

6 sun-ripened tomatoes, peeled
and chopped

1 bay leaf

pepper

1 sprig fresh thyme

1 sprig parsley

⅓ cup/40 g/1½ oz fresh
breadcrumbs (optional)

lemon slices

SERVES 6

Spread the eggplant slices on a cloth and sprinkle with
salt. Let stand for 10 minutes, then rinse and dry thoroughly. Fry the potatoes in the oil until golden. Remove.
Fry eggplant until the surfaces are well sealed. Remove
and overlap in a pie dish with sloping sides. Fry the
peppers until softened; remove. Briefly fry the garlic.
Layer the vegetables in the pie dish and set aside.

Fry the chopped onion in the same pan until softened.
Add the tomatoes, seasonings and herbs and cook to a
pulp. Pour over the vegetables. If you do not wish to
invert the dish, fry the breadcrumbs in olive oil and
sprinkle over the top of the vegetables. Bake in a preheated 400°F/200°C/Gas 6 oven for 15 to 20 minutes.
Allow to set for a few minutes, then invert onto a serving
plate and garnish with slices of lemon. Serve hot or, if
preferred, allow to cool to room temperature.

ESPINACAS A LA CATALANA
SPINACH WITH PINE NUTS AND RAISINS

2 lb/1 kg fresh spinach

⅓ cup/45 g/1½ oz pine nuts

½ cup/90 g/3 oz raisins

¼ cup/60 ml/2 fl oz olive oil

¾ teaspoon salt

freshly ground black pepper

SERVES 4–6

Break off spinach stems and discard. Wash leaves thoroughly and shake to dry. Place in a covered saucepan and cook over low heat for 5 minutes or until softened. Drain well. Fry the nuts and raisins in olive oil until the raisins are plump and nuts are golden. Add spinach and toss quickly over high heat. Season and serve at once.

SAMFAINA
CATALAN BRAISED VEGETABLE SAUCE

4 large red bell peppers
(capsicums)

½ cup/120 ml/4 fl oz extra-virgin
olive oil

2 large onions, very thinly sliced

1 large purple or several small
Japanese eggplants (aubergines),
about 12 oz/350 g

4 medium zucchini (courgettes),
about 1 lb/500 g, cubed

4 cloves garlic, minced

3–4 large sun-ripened tomatoes,
peeled, seeded and finely chopped

salt and pepper

MAKES 3–3½ CUPS

Roast the peppers on a grill or in a hot oven until the surface is blackened, turning frequently. Wrap in a kitchen towel for 10 minutes, then peel. Discard seeds and cut flesh into narrow strips. Heat the oil in a heavy pan. Add the onions, eggplant, zucchini and garlic. Stir to coat with the oil, then cover and cook gently for about 10 minutes. Uncover and cook over higher heat to evaporate the pan liquids. Add the peppers and tomato and cook uncovered over low heat until the vegetables are all very soft. Season to taste.

PARRILLADA DE MARISCOS
CATALAN-STYLE SEAFOOD GRILL

salt

6 thick pieces hake, about 4 oz/
120 g each

6 whiting fillets

6 *cigalas* (scampi/Dublin Bay
prawns/langoustines)

6 *langostinos* (large shrimp/
prawns) in their shells

12 clams in their shells, soaked
overnight

12 large oysters on the half shell

olive oil

finely chopped garlic (optional)

lemons

SERVES 6

Prepare a good bed of glowing charcoal under an iron grill. Sprinkle salt over the fish and let stand for 10 minutes, then brush with olive oil. If you like, cut the *langostinos* down the center backs to extract the dark vein. Brush shellfish with oil. Place the seafood on the grill to cook until tender, turning several times; cooking time will depend on the size of the pieces. Add oysters last as they need only a few minutes to heat.

Separately heat a small pot of good olive oil, adding garlic. Pour over the seafood when it has been arranged on plates and garnish with lemon wedges.

PESCADO A L'ALL CREMAT
FISH IN BURNT GARLIC

1 large head garlic, slivered

$\frac{1}{3}$ cup/90 ml/3 fl oz olive oil

3 large sun-ripened tomatoes,
seeded and chopped

1 sprig fresh thyme

1 bay leaf

1$\frac{1}{2}$ lb/750 g cod, sea bream or bass
fillets

salt and pepper

SERVES 4

In a flameproof *cazuela* or casserole, slowly brown the garlic in the oil until very dark. Add the tomatoes with herbs and cook, stirring, until thickened, then add enough water to moisten. Lay the fish on the sauce. Season lightly, sprinkle on a little olive oil to keep the fish moist, then cover and cook gently, turning once, until fish is tender. Serve in the casserole.

31

Pollo al Ajillo
GARLIC CHICKEN

12 oz/380 g boneless chicken
breast, skin on

5–6 cloves garlic, slivered

3 tablespoons olive oil

salt

$\frac{1}{2}$ cup/120 ml/4 fl oz dry white
wine (optional)

2 teaspoons chopped parsley

SERVES 4

Cut the chicken into strips across the fillet. Sauté chicken and garlic in the oil over low heat until the chicken is tender and the garlic has thoroughly impregnated the meat. Add salt to taste. Splash in the wine, if used, and increase the heat until the wine is absorbed. Sprinkle on the parsley and serve.

Chuletas de Cerdo en Salsa de Granadas
PORK CUTLETS IN POMEGRANATE SAUCE

2 tablespoons lard or butter

4 pork chops, about 180 g/6 oz
each

1 large onion, sliced

2 ripe pomegranates

$\frac{1}{2}$ cup/120 ml/4 fl oz dry white
wine

$\frac{1}{2}$ cup/120 ml/4 fl oz veal or
chicken stock

salt and pepper

SERVES 4

Heat the lard or butter in a wide pan, add the chops and cook on both sides until well browned. Remove and keep warm. Pour off half the fat. Sauté onion until golden and softened.

Meanwhile, cut pomegranates in half and scoop out the seeds and pulp. Add to the pan with the wine and cook for 5 minutes. Transfer to a baking dish with the chops, stock and salt and pepper to taste. Cover and bake in a preheated 350°F/180°C/Gas 4 oven for about 40 minutes or until the pork is completely tender.

PA I ALL
GARLIC BREAD

4–5 cloves garlic, smoothly mashed

8 slices crusty country bread

$\frac{1}{4}$ cup/60 ml/2 fl oz virgin or extra-virgin olive oil

salt

SERVES 4

Spread the garlic over one side of the bread and drizzle with enough olive oil to moisten without turning the bread soggy. Season to taste.

POLVORONES
ALMOND SHORTBREAD

1 cup/150 g/5 oz blanched almonds

2 cups/250 g/8 oz all-purpose (plain) flour

2 teaspoons cinnamon

$\frac{1}{3}$ teaspoon salt

1$\frac{1}{3}$ cups/350 g/11 oz butter or lard

$\frac{1}{2}$ cup/120 g/4 oz sugar

1 egg

$\frac{1}{4}$ cup/60 ml/2 fl oz Cointreau or Grand Marnier

confectioners' (icing) sugar

MAKES ABOUT 36

Spread the almonds on a baking sheet and toast in a moderate oven for about 25 minutes to a rich golden brown. Allow to cool, then grind to a fine powder in a food processor or mortar. Sift the flour, cinnamon and salt into a bowl. Add the almonds and stir in well. Cream butter or lard with sugar until smooth and light, then stir in the egg and liqueur. Work into the flour to make a crumbly dough.

Roll dough out to $\frac{3}{4}$-inch/2-cm thickness on a lightly floured board and cut into small oval shapes. Use a spatula to transfer to a greased and floured baking sheet and prick lightly a few times with a fork. Bake in a preheated 325°F/160°C/Gas 3 oven for about 20 minutes or until light golden. Cool on a wire rack. Coat with confectioners' sugar and wrap in squares of tissue paper.

ARAGON

LENGUA A LA ARAGONESA

TONGUE IN PEPPER TOMATO SAUCE

1 2-lb/1-kg ox tongue or 2–3
calves' tongues, soaked overnight
if salted

2 medium onions, peeled

1 medium carrot, peeled

1 bay leaf

2 sprigs fresh thyme

2 sprigs parsley

1 sprig fresh oregano

3 tablespoons olive oil

4 cloves garlic, finely chopped

2 large red bell peppers
(capsicums), seeded and sliced

4 large sun-ripened tomatoes,
peeled, seeded and chopped

$\frac{1}{4}$ cup/60 ml/2 fl oz dry sherry

6–8 saffron threads, crushed

$\frac{1}{4}$ cup/60 ml/2 fl oz boiling water

$\frac{1}{2}$ teaspoon hot paprika

salt and pepper

SERVES 6

Place the tongue/s in a large saucepan with water to cover generously. Add one onion, quartered, the carrot, bay leaf, thyme, parsley and oregano and bring to a boil. Reduce heat and simmer for $2\frac{1}{2}$ to 4 hours or until the tongue/s can be easily pierced with a skewer. Remove and drain, then strip off the skin. Place tongue in a bowl and put a weight on top. Refrigerate for at least 4 hours, preferably overnight.

Finely chop the other onion and sauté in the oil until lightly colored. Add the garlic and peppers and cook 3 to 4 minutes, then add tomatoes and cook until soft. Process to a creamy consistency in a blender or food processor and return to the pan. Add sherry and saffron, which has been dissolved in the boiling water. Simmer briefly, add paprika and check seasoning. To serve hot, slice the tongue, warm in the sauce and serve with boiled potatoes. Or serve cold by slicing the tongue and arranging on a platter dressed with onion rings and parsley. Serve the sauce separately at room temperature.

HABAS CON SALCHICHAS
BEANS WITH SAUSAGES

1 medium onion, very finely
chopped

3 tablespoons olive oil

4 large sun-ripened tomatoes,
peeled, seeded and chopped

2½ lb/1.2 kg fresh broadbeans,
peeled

salt and pepper

1 tablespoon finely chopped
parsley

lemon juice

4–8 spicy pork sausages

SERVES 4

Sauté the onion in the oil until golden, add the tomatoes and cook for 2 to 3 minutes. Add the beans, salt and pepper, cover tightly and simmer over low heat until the beans are tender, 15 to 30 minutes depending on their age. Stir in the parsley and sprinkle on a little lemon juice. In the meantime, prick the sausages and cook on a griddle or in a frying pan with a very little oil or lard until cooked through and golden brown. Spread the beans on plates and arrange the sausages on top.

TRUCHAS CON VINO Y ROMERO
TROUT WITH RED WINE AND ROSEMARY

4 freshwater trout

2 tablespoons olive oil

salt and pepper

1 clove garlic, mashed

4 sprigs fresh rosemary

¾ cup/180 ml/6 fl oz red wine

2 teaspoons chopped fresh mint

SERVES 4

Clean the trout and rinse well. Rub with the oil, salt and pepper. Season the cavity with salt, pepper and garlic and place a sprig of rosemary inside each fish. Pour remaining oil into an oven dish and arrange the fish side by side in it. Add the wine and season with salt and pepper. Cover and bake in a preheated 350°F/180°C/Gas 4 oven for about 18 minutes or until the fish can be easily flaked with a fork. Sprinkle with mint and serve.

NAVARRA AND LA RIOJA

MENESTRA TUDELANA
VEGETABLE CASSEROLE TUDELA STYLE

12 baby artichokes

lemon juice or vinegar

2 lb/1 kg fresh broadbeans in the
shell (or 12 oz/350 g beans)

2–3 cloves garlic, finely chopped

3 tablespoons olive oil

1 tablespoon ground almonds

$\frac{1}{3}$ cup/90 ml/3 fl oz dry white wine

1 sprig fresh thyme

salt and pepper

1 cup/250 ml/8 fl oz water

5 saffron threads

2 teaspoons chopped fresh mint
(optional)

4 hard-boiled eggs, cut into
wedges

SERVES 4

Trim off the outer leaves and tips of the artichokes.
Place artichokes in a non-aluminum pot of cold water
acidulated with a little lemon juice or vinegar. Bring to
a boil and simmer for 5 minutes, then drain. Boil broadbeans separately in lightly salted water for about
5 minutes. Sauté the garlic in olive oil for 1 minute. Add
the ground almonds, artichokes and broadbeans and
sauté together for a further minute. Add the wine and
thyme with salt and pepper to taste and cook until the
wine evaporates. Add the water, cover and simmer for
about 20 minutes. Crush saffron and dissolve in a little
of the hot liquid from the pot; stir into the vegetables.
Add mint and the eggs, warm through and serve.

Lengua a la Aragonesa (recipe page 34)

Above, Lacón con Grelos (recipe page 50);
below, Pulpo á Feira (recipe page 50)

PATATAS A LA RIOJANA
POTATOES WITH PAPRIKA AND CHORIZO

4 large potatoes, peeled and
thickly sliced

$\frac{1}{4}$ cup/60 ml/2 fl oz olive oil

8 oz/250 g *chorizo* sausage

1 medium onion, thinly sliced

1 clove garlic, finely chopped

2 teaspoons sweet paprika

1 small hot red chili pepper,
seeded and chopped

$1\frac{1}{2}$ cups/400 ml/13 fl oz cold water

salt and pepper

SERVES 4

Sauté the potatoes in the oil until lightly colored. Remove
and set aside. Fry the whole sausages in the remaining
oil until the surface is crisp; remove. Sauté the onion
and garlic until golden. Slice the sausage and return to
the pan with the paprika and chili. Cook briefly, then
add the potatoes with water and salt and pepper to
taste. Cover tightly and cook until the potatoes are
tender.

TRUCHAS A LA NAVARRA
TROUT NAVARRE STYLE

4 freshwater trout (about 12 oz/
350 g each), cleaned

salt and black pepper

1 tablespoon lemon juice

4 long, thin slices *jamón serrano* or
other cured ham

$\frac{1}{3}$ cup/45 g/1$\frac{1}{2}$ oz all-purpose (plain)
flour

$\frac{1}{2}$ cup/120 ml/4 fl oz olive oil

lemon wedges

SERVES 4

Rinse the trout and dry well. Season inside the cavity
with salt, pepper and lemon juice and lightly salt and
pepper the outside. Place a folded slice of ham in the
cavity of each fish, or wrap around the fish and tie loosely
with thin string. Coat lightly with flour. Heat oil in a
large skillet or sauté pan and fry the fish on both sides
until well browned and cooked through. Remove the
string and transfer fish to a warmed serving plate. Serve
with lemon wedges.

Brochetas de Solomillo a la Riojana
TENDERLOIN BROCHETTES

2 lb/1 kg beef tenderloin

2 cloves garlic, mashed

$\frac{3}{4}$ teaspoon salt

$\frac{1}{2}$ teaspoon sweet paprika

black pepper

1 cup/250 ml/8 fl oz dry red wine

1 bay leaf

1 sprig fresh thyme or rosemary

2 tablespoons olive oil

SERVES 4–6

Cut the beef into 1-inch/2.5-cm cubes and thread onto metal skewers. Mix garlic, salt, paprika and pepper and rub over the meat. Place in a flat dish and pour on the wine. Add bay leaf and herbs and marinate for 2 hours, turning several times.

Remove skewers from the marinade and drain. Brush with oil and cook over glowing charcoal until crisped on the surface but still tender inside. Serve with potatoes.

Cochifrito de Cordero
LAMB SAUTÉED WITH GARLIC AND LEMON

$1\frac{1}{2}$ lb/750 g lean lamb, diced

2–3 tablespoons olive oil

1 large onion, chopped

3 cloves garlic, minced

$\frac{3}{4}$ teaspoon sweet paprika

1 tablespoon lemon juice

salt and pepper

2 teaspoons chopped parsley

SERVES 4

Sauté the lamb in hot oil until well browned; remove and keep warm. Sauté the onion until golden brown and softened. Push to one side of the pan, add the garlic and paprika and sauté for 1 minute. Return the meat, add lemon juice and cook, stirring continually, for 4 to 6 minutes or until the meat is cooked, adding salt and pepper to taste. Sprinkle on the parsley and serve hot.

BASQUE COUNTRY

SHANGURRO AL HORNO
BASQUE STUFFED CRABS

4 cooked crabs, 1–1½ lbs/500–750 g each

OR 1 lb/500 g crabmeat (Alaskan king crab is best)

1 large onion, very finely chopped

1 small carrot, peeled and grated

2 tablespoons olive oil

1 clove garlic, finely chopped

½ small hot red chili pepper, seeded and finely chopped

1 teaspoon sweet paprika

1 large tomato, peeled, seeded and chopped

1 teaspoon tomato paste

½ cup/120 ml/4 fl oz dry white wine

2 tablespoons Spanish brandy or dry sherry

1 tablespoon finely chopped parsley

salt and pepper

⅓ cup/45 g/1½ oz fine dry breadcrumbs

1 tablespoon butter

SERVES 4

Cut away the undersides of the crabs, separate meat from the inedible parts and flake. Extract the *tomalley* and set aside with the crabmeat. Scrape and clean the shells; place in a baking dish. Crack claws and extract the flesh. Sauté the onion and carrot in oil for 5 minutes. Add the garlic, chili and paprika and sauté briefly, then add the tomato and tomato paste and cook, stirring occasionally, for about 3 minutes. Add wine and brandy, the crabmeat, parsley, salt and pepper. Cook for 3 to 4 minutes. Stir in the *tomalley*. Pile into the prepared crab shells and smooth the tops. Sprinkle breadcrumbs evenly over the filling and dot with butter. Bake crabs in a preheated 400°F/200°C/Gas 6 oven until the tops brown, about 12 minutes. Serve at once with a green salad.

Sopa de Pescado
BASQUE FISH SOUP

$2\frac{1}{4}$ lb/1.2 kg assorted small fish

3 lb/1.5 kg assorted shellfish

olive oil

1 large onion, finely chopped

3–6 cloves garlic, finely chopped

1 large carrot, peeled and diced

1 cup/250 ml/8 fl oz dry white wine

3 slices white bread, crusts trimmed

1 bouquet garni, or sprigs of fresh herbs

salt and pepper

SERVES 6–8

Clean the fish, leaving them whole, and rinse well in cold water. Drain and dry. Thoroughly scrub the shellfish and place in a saucepan. Cover and cook without liquid over low heat, shaking the pan to encourage the shells to open. Remove from heat, remove the top section of each shell and discard those which have not opened. Set aside, reserving any liquid in the pan. Fry the fish in oil for 2 to 3 minutes, then transfer to a deep pan and add 4 cups/1 l/32 fl oz water. Bring almost to a boil and simmer 8 minutes. Remove the fish and separate meat from bones. Break meat into bite-size pieces. Strain the stock and reserve, discarding fish carcasses, heads and bones. Fry the onion, garlic and carrot in olive oil for 3 minutes. Add the wine and heat to boiling, cooking for 2 minutes. Add the bread and 4 cups/1 l/32 fl oz water, bring to a boil and simmer for 15 minutes, then strain through a fine sieve. Push vegetables and bread through the sieve, discarding any that will not pass through. Return the shellfish to the soup and add the herbs, seasonings and reserved shellfish liquid. Bring almost to a boil, then reduce heat and simmer slowly for about 4 minutes. Add the fish and reserved fish stock and heat thoroughly. Season with salt and pepper. Float a little olive oil on top and serve at once.

Variation: If a thicker, more textured soup is preferred, do not sieve the bread and vegetables; soak the bread first in cold water, squeeze and cut into small pieces.

BACALAO A LA VIZCAÍNA
BAY OF BISCAY SALT COD WITH ONIONS AND RED PEPPERS

$1\frac{1}{2}$ lb/750 g prepared *bacalao* (page 380)

2 medium onions, chopped

4 cloves garlic, minced

2–3 tablespoons olive oil

1 medium potato, peeled and finely chopped

6 dried hot red chili peppers (chillies), soaked for 10 hours, or 1–2 chili peppers and 1 red bell pepper (capsicum)

4 large tomatoes, peeled, seeded and chopped

2 slices toasted bread, crusts trimmed

1 bay leaf

1 sprig parsley

salt and pepper

$\frac{1}{2}$ cup/30 g/1 oz fresh white breadcrumbs

butter or oil

chopped parsley

SERVES 4

Place the cod in a saucepan with water just to cover. Simmer for 20 minutes. Discard any bones and reserve the liquid. Sauté the onions and garlic in the olive oil for 3 minutes; add the potato and sauté for 3 minutes. Slit open the chili peppers and discard the seeds. Cut peppers into fine shreds and cook with the onion and tomato until a soft purée. Add $\frac{1}{2}$ cup/120 ml/4 fl oz reserved fish stock and bread and simmer until mixture is reduced to a pulp. Purée sauce in a food processor and strain. Pour half the sauce into a casserole and place the fish on top, skin side up. Add the bay leaf, parsley, salt and pepper. Cover loosely and bake in a preheated 350°F/ 180°C/Gas 4 oven for about 20 minutes or until fairly dry. Uncover, sprinkle with breadcrumbs and moisten with butter or oil. Bake a further 10 minutes, then sprinkle with parsley and serve.

Tip: There are many interpretations of this classic dish. In one popular version, the onions, peppers, garlic and bread are cooked together briefly, then added in chunky form to the casserole. The dish is stirred several times during cooking. Breadcrumbs on top can be omitted, or replaced by a sprinkling of garlic fried in oil.

BACALAO PREPARATION

Soak dried salt cod for 24 to 48 hours in cold water to cover generously, changing the water several times. Alternatively, soak overnight in cold water, drain, cover with fresh water and bring to a boil. Drain and repeat twice. Drain the fish and pull away the skin and any remaining bones (use tweezers if necessary).

At this stage the fish will be completely rehydrated, only slightly salty and ready for cooking.

PIPERRADA

BASQUE PEPPER CASSEROLE WITH EGG AND TOMATO

2 red bell peppers (capsicums)

2 green bell peppers (capsicums)

$\frac{1}{2}$ cup/120 ml/4 fl oz olive oil

4–5 large sun-ripened tomatoes, peeled, seeded and chopped

4 oz/250 g *jamón serrano* or other cured ham, sliced

1–3 cloves garlic, minced

1–2 teaspoons chopped fresh basil

salt and pepper

4 eggs, beaten

SERVES 4

Drop the peppers into a pot of boiling water and cook until the skins loosen, about 4 minutes. Skin, seed and cut the flesh into strips. Sauté in the oil for at least 20 minutes or until well softened. Add the tomatoes and cook for 10 minutes. Very finely shred the ham and add to the pan with the garlic, basil, salt and pepper. Cook, stirring frequently, until the mixture is soft and pulpy. Add the egg a little at a time, stirring, until the mixture is smooth and fluffy. Spoon onto warmed plates and serve at once.

OLD CASTILE AND LEON

LENTEJAS CON CHORIZO EN CAZUELA
CASSEROLE OF LENTILS AND CHORIZO

2 cups/350 g/12 oz red or yellow lentils

3 oz/90 g salted *tocino* or other salt pork, diced

1 medium onion, chopped

3 cloves garlic, chopped

$\frac{1}{4}$ cup/60 ml/2 fl oz olive oil

3 sun-ripened tomatoes, chopped

8 oz/250 g *chorizo* sausage

1 tablespoon finely chopped fresh herbs

salt and pepper

1 teaspoon sweet paprika

12 saffron threads (optional)

SERVES 4–6

Rinse the lentils in cold water and drain. In a heavy-bottomed saucepan sauté the salt pork, onion and garlic in the oil for a few minutes. Add the tomatoes and cook for 5 minutes, then add the lentils and whole *chorizo* sausage. Add the herbs and seasonings with water to cover by about 1½ inches/4 cm. Bring to a boil, cover and cook gently for about 30 minutes or until the lentils are tender, check the quantity of water after 20 minutes; the dish should remain moist but not liquid. Remove the *chorizo*, slice and return to the pot. Grind the saffron and dissolve in 2 tablespoons boiling water. Add to the pot with additional salt and pepper as needed.

COCHINILLO ASADO Á FEIRA

FESTIVE ROAST SUCKLING PIG

6- to 7-lb/3- to 3½-kg suckling pig

2 tablespoons crushed sea salt

½ cup/120 ml/4 fl oz oil or melted lard

4 oz/120 g *chorizo* sausage

12 oz/350 g pork sausages

1 medium onion, very finely chopped

2 cloves garlic, chopped

2 tablespoons olive oil

1 young pig's liver, very finely chopped

2 teaspoons finely chopped fresh herbs

1 tablespoon finely chopped parsley

grated rind of ½ lemon or orange

2 cups/120 g/4 oz fresh breadcrumbs

1 egg

salt and pepper

SERVES 8

Pour boiling water over the skin of the pig, which helps it to turn crisp when cooked. Drain well, then rub with salt and oil or lard. Remove the sausage meat from its casings. Sauté the onion and garlic in the oil until lightly colored. Combine with the remaining ingredients and blend well. Stuff into the cavity of the pig and secure the opening with wooden or metal skewers. Place the pig on a rack in a roasting pan. Roast in a preheated 425°F/220°C/Gas 7 oven for 15 minutes. Reduce the heat to 375°F/190°C/Gas 5. Baste the pig and roast a further 45 minutes. Increase the heat to 425°F/200°C/Gas 7 for a final 30 to 45 minutes cooking, basting frequently with the pan juices. Protect vulnerable areas from overcooking by masking with pieces of aluminum foil. Remove the pig and let stand for 10 minutes before carving. Skim the pan drippings of excess fat, whisk in a little flour and stock and boil to thicken to gravy consistency. Serve with the pig.

GALLINA EN PEPITORIA
CHICKEN IN SAFFRON SAUCE

1.5-kg/3-lb chicken

salt and pepper

$\frac{3}{4}$ cup/90 g/3 oz all-purpose (plain)
flour

$\frac{1}{3}$ cup/90 ml/3 fl oz olive oil

2 large onions, finely chopped

4 cloves garlic, finely chopped

2 bay leaves

1 cup/250 ml/8 fl oz dry white
wine

$1\frac{3}{4}$ cups/450 ml/14 fl oz chicken
stock

$\frac{3}{4}$ cup/80 g/$2\frac{1}{2}$ oz ground almonds

10 threads saffron

chopped parsley

SERVES 4

Cut chicken into serving portions, season with salt and pepper and coat lightly with flour. Fry in the oil for about 10 minutes until well colored, then remove and pour off most of the oil. Fry the onions until golden and soft; add garlic and bay leaves and fry briefly. Add wine, stock, ground almonds and chicken, cover and cook over low heat for about 20 minutes, stirring occasionally to keep the sauce from sticking to the pan.

Wrap saffron in a small square of aluminum foil and toast for 2 to 3 minutes in a dry pan. Grind in a mortar, then add 2 to 3 tablespoons boiling water, stir well and pour over the dish. Cook a further 15 minutes. Transfer to a serving dish and sprinkle with parsley.

HIGOS CON MIEL
FIGS IN HONEY

18–24 plump dried figs

2 cups/500 ml/16 fl oz ruby port

1 cup/250 ml/8 fl oz orange juice

$\frac{1}{3}$ cup/90 g/3 oz clear honey

whipped cream

SERVES 6

Stem the figs and place in a wide non-aluminum pan. Add the port, orange juice and honey and bring almost to a boil. Reduce heat and simmer for about 45 minutes.

Serve hot or cold with whipped cream.

Fabada Asturiana

2 cups/350 g/12 oz butter beans
or lima beans (or use Boston/
haricot/navy beans)

1 ham/bacon hock

1 pork hock/pig's foot/trotter

6 oz/180 g salted *tocino*, salt pork
or bacon

1 lb/500 g fresh bacon/belly pork,
sliced

4 pieces (about 1¼ lb/650 g) veal
shank/shin

12 oz/350 g *chorizo* sausages

10 oz/300 g *morcilla* or other
blood sausages

1 large onion, thinly sliced

1 whole head garlic, peeled

1 dried hot red chili pepper

2 bay leaves

2 sprigs fresh thyme

SERVES 8

Rinse the beans and drain; place in a very large pot with the ham or bacon hock and pork hock. Cover with water and bring to the boil. Simmer for 10 minutes, then drain. Cover with warm fresh water, adding the bacon, sliced pork and veal pieces. Bring to a boil and simmer for 1 hour. Add the sausages, onion, garlic, chili and herbs and simmer slowly for another 1½ hours, adding warm water from time to time as needed.

Remove the ham and pork hocks, pick off any meat and return it to the pot. Discard veal marrow bones, if preferred. Slice the *tocino* and sausages or leave whole as desired. Serve in a deep dish with plenty of crusty bread.

Tip: Like many stewed dishes *fabada* improves with keeping, so prepare in advance and reheat.

CALDERETA DE PESCADO Y MARISCOS

CASSEROLE OF FISH AND SHELLFISH

2-lb/1-kg bream (sea bass)

1 lb/500 g hake, halibut or cod
fillets

6 fresh squid

6 fresh mussels in the shell

12 fresh clams in the shell

12 medium shrimp (prawns) in
the shell

6 *cigalas* (saltwater crayfish/
Dublin Bay prawns)

1 medium onion, chopped

$\frac{1}{3}$ cup/90 ml/3 fl oz olive oil

1 medium-size red bell pepper
(capsicum), seeded and chopped

2 large sun-ripened tomatoes,
seeded and chopped

1 dried hot red chili pepper

2 bay leaves

2 sprigs fresh parsley

5 black peppercorns

$\frac{1}{3}$ teaspoon powdered saffron

SERVES 6–8

Place the bream and hake in a large pan and add water just to cover. Simmer for 4 minutes, then carefully remove and pick the flesh from the bones. Return bones and head to the pot and cook another 6 minutes, then strain stock into a jug. Clean squid and cut into rings. Rinse the pan and put in all of the shellfish. Add 4 cups/ 1 l/32 fl oz cold water and bring to a boil. Shake the pan over moderate heat for 3 to 4 minutes until the shells open. Remove from the heat. Strain the liquid into the jug with the fish stock. Discard any shellfish that do not open and remove the top shell from each of the shellfish. Peel shrimp and *cigalas*. Rinse pan again and fry the onion in oil until lightly colored and soft. Add pepper and fry briefly, then add tomato and remaining ingredients except saffron and cook for 3 to 4 minutes. Add the strained stock and saffron and bring to a boil; simmer for 5 to 6 minutes. Return all of the seafood and heat through for 3 to 4 minutes before serving with plenty of crusty bread.

Estofado de Buey a la Asturiana

BRAISED BEEF WITH VEGETABLES

$1\frac{1}{2}$ lb/750 g lean, cubed round beef

$\frac{1}{2}$ cup/120 ml/4 fl oz olive oil

1 large onion, chopped

3 cloves garlic, chopped

2 oz/60 g salted *tocino*, salt pork or bacon, diced

1 medium carrot, peeled and diced

1 cup/250 ml/8 fl oz red or dry white wine

3 tablespoons brandy or dry sherry

2-inch/5-cm cinnamon stick

1 bay leaf

1 sprig each fresh thyme, parsley and sage

1 teaspoon sweet paprika

12 small new potatoes, peeled

12 baby turnips, peeled

12 small (pickling) onions, peeled

salt and pepper

SERVES 4–6

Fry the beef in the oil over high heat until all surfaces are seared. Remove and keep warm. Fry the onion until well colored. Add the garlic, *tocino* and carrot and fry for 2 minutes. Add wine and brandy and cook over high heat until reduced by half. Return the meat and add the spices and herbs. Add $1\frac{1}{2}$ cups/400 ml/13 fl oz warm water and bring to a boil. Cover and cook very slowly for $1\frac{1}{4}$ hours. Add the vegetables and season with salt and pepper, then cook another 15 minutes or until tender. If necessary, remove the meat and vegetables with a slotted spoon and boil the sauce rapidly to reduce, or stir in a little flour mixed to a paste with a teaspoon of butter to thicken. If the stew is too dry, add a little warm water during cooking.

Tip: *Estofado* is greatly improved if prepared a day in advance and reheated. The Catalonians enjoy a slightly sweet and crunchy variation of this dish by adding previously boiled prunes half an hour before serving, and a handful of toasted pine nuts at the last minute.

Patatas a la Riojana (recipe page 37);
center left, Brochetas de Solomillo a la Riojana (recipe page 38);
top right, Menestra Tudelana (recipe page 36)

Caldereta de Pescado y Mariscos (recipe page 47)

GALICIA

CALDO GALLEGO
GALICIAN BROTH

1 cup/180 g/6 oz haricot (navy)
beans, soaked overnight

6 oz/180 g *chorizo* sausages

1 ham (bacon) hock

3 thick slices (about 200 g/7 oz)
smoked bacon or ham

8 cups/2 1/2¹ qt water or beef/veal
stock

1 lb/500 g potatoes, peeled and
cubed

2 medium turnips, peeled and
chopped

1 medium onion, chopped

1 large carrot, peeled and chopped

2 cups/200 g/7 oz chopped
cabbage

2 cups/200 g/7 oz chopped turnip
or other greens

3 cloves garlic, chopped

salt and pepper

SERVES 6–8

Place beans, whole *chorizo*, ham hock and sliced ham in a pot with the water. Bring to a boil and reduce heat; simmer for 2½ hours, skimming the surface from time to time. Remove meat. Slice sausage, remove ham from hock and chop, dice the smoked ham, and return to the pot. Add vegetables and garlic and continue to simmer until they have become very tender and are starting to break up and thicken the broth, adding more water or beef/veal stock as needed. Check for seasoning, adding salt and pepper. Serve hot with warm, crusty rolls.

Tip: A little virgin olive oil floated on the surface of the soup adds extra flavor and is said to aid digestion.

PULPO Á FEIRA
OCTOPUS FESTIVE STYLE

3-lb/1.5-kg octopus (or use the same weight of baby octopus)

5–8 cloves garlic, finely chopped

2½ teaspoons sweet paprika

salt and pepper

½ cup/120 ml/4 fl oz olive oil

chopped fresh herbs (parsley, dill)

1 medium onion, sliced

SERVES 6 (*TAPA*)

Turn the body part of the octopus inside out and trim away the inedible parts, then cut away eyes and mouth sections. Rinse thoroughly. Place the octopus in a heavy saucepan with 1 cup/250 ml/8 fl oz water, cover tightly and cook over very low heat for about 1½ hours or until it is tender enough to be easily pierced with a knife. (Small octopus does not require water and will be tender in about 35 minutes.)

Remove the pan from the heat and set aside until completely cold. Drain octopus and rinse under running cold water, rubbing off any fragments of skin. Cut into bite-size serving pieces. Mix the garlic, seasonings and oil and pour over. Garnish with chopped fresh herbs and onion rings and serve cold.

LACÓN CON GRELOS
PORK WITH TURNIP GREENS

3 lb/1.5 kg *lacón* (smoked/salted foreleg of pork)*

12 oz/350 g *chorizo* sausages, cubed

2lb/1 kg *grelos*, beet greens, silver-beet or mustard greens, lower stems removed, leaves chopped

salt and pepper

4 medium potatoes, peeled and cubed

SERVES 6–8

Place the pork in a large pan with water to cover. Bring to a boil and reduce heat. Cook for 1½ hours. Add *chorizo* and *grelos* with salt and pepper to taste. Cook a further 30 minutes. Add potatoes and simmer gently until they begin to break up. Adjust seasoning. Serve in a deep dish with crusty bread.

* Pickled or salted pork can replace *lacón*.